Western
Great Lakes

Illinois
Minnesota
Wisconsin

Mason Crest
450 Parkway Drive, Suite D
Broomall, PA 19008
www.masoncrest.com

©2016 by Mason Crest, an imprint of National Highlights, Inc.

Printed and bound in the United States of America.

CPSIA Compliance Information: Batch #LES2015.
For further information, contact Mason Crest at 1-866-MCP-Book.

First printing
1 3 5 7 9 8 6 4 2

Library of Congress Cataloging-in-Publication Data

Ziff, John.
  Western Great Lakes : Illinois, Minnesota, Wisconsin / John Ziff.
      pages cm. — (Let's explore the states)
  Includes bibliographical references and index.
  ISBN 978-1-4222-3338-2 (hc)
  ISBN 978-1-4222-8623-4 (ebook)
  1. Lake States—Juvenile literature. 2. Illinois—Juvenile literature. 3. Minnesota—Juvenile literature. 4. Wisconsin—Juvenile literature. I. Title.
  F551.Z49 2015
  977—dc23
                              2014050188

Let's Explore the States series ISBN: 978-1-4222-3319-1

Publisher's Note: Websites listed in this book were active at the time of publication. The publisher is not responsible for websites that have changed their address or discontinued operation since the date of publication. The publisher reviews and updates the websites each time the book is reprinted.

About the Author: John Ziff is an editor and writer. He lives near Philadelphia.

Picture Credits: courtesy General Mills: 36; Library of Congress, 14, 15, 20 (top right), 33, 34, 51, 52, 58 (top, bottom); Bruce Marlin: 18 (bottom); National Archives, 13; used under license from Shutterstock, Inc.: 6, 9, 10, 11, 16, 17, 18 (top), 24, 27, 28, 29, 31, 32, 37, 38, 40, 42, 43, 46, 49, 54, 55 (top), 56, 57, 60; Beelde Photography/Shutterstock, 58 (center); John Brueske/Shutterstock: 5 (top); Karla Caspari/Shutterstock: 30; Richard Cavalleri/Shutterstock: 21; Anthony Correia/Shutterstock: 39 (left); Helga Esteb/Shutterstock, 20 (bottom right); D. Free/Shutterstock: 39 (right); Nancy Gill/Shutterstock: 5 (bottom); Allison Herreid/Shutterstock: 50; Mark Herreid/Shutterstock: 61 (bottom); Michael Holcomb/Shutterstock: 35 (bottom right); Eugene Moerman/Shutterstock: 1; Al Mueller/Shutterstock: 35 (top right); Pecold/Shutterstock: 45; Photo.ua/Shutterstock: 44; Jason Patrick Ross/Shutterstock: 53; Joseph Scott Photography/Shutterstock: 41; Lorraine Swanson/Shutterstock: 61 (top); Dan Thornberg/Shutterstock: 26; Suzanne Tucker/Shutterstock: 59; Lynn Watson/Shutterstock: 19; Katherine Welles/Shutterstock: 55 (bottom); Gary Yim/Shutterstock: 22; Spirit of America: 20 (left); U.S. Congress: 35 (top left).

Table of Contents

KEY ICONS TO LOOK FOR:

 Words to Understand: These words with their easy-to-understand definitions will increase the reader's understanding of the text, while building vocabulary skills.

 Sidebars: This boxed material within the main text allows readers to build knowledge, gain insights, explore possibilities, and broaden their perspectives by weaving together additional information to provide realistic and holistic perspectives.

 Research Projects: Readers are pointed toward areas of further inquiry connected to each chapter. Suggestions are provided for projects that encourage deeper research and analysis.

 Text-Dependent Questions: These questions send the reader back to the text for more careful attention to the evidence presented there.

 Series Glossary of Key Terms: This back-of-the book glossary contains terminology used throughout this series. Words found here increase the reader's ability to read and comprehend higher-level books and articles in this field.

LET'S EXPLORE THE STATES

Atlantic: North Carolina, Virginia, West Virginia

Central Mississippi River Basin: Arkansas, Iowa, Missouri

East South-Central States: Kentucky, Tennessee

Eastern Great Lakes: Indiana, Michigan, Ohio

Gulf States: Alabama, Louisiana, Mississippi

Lower Atlantic: Florida, Georgia, South Carolina

Lower Plains: Kansas, Nebraska

Mid-Atlantic: Delaware, District of Columbia, Maryland

Non-Continental: Alaska, Hawaii

Northern New England: Maine, New Hampshire, Vermont

Northeast: New Jersey, New York, Pennsylvania

Northwest: Idaho, Oregon, Washington

Rocky Mountain: Colorado, Utah, Wyoming

Southern New England: Connecticut, Massachusetts, Rhode Island

Southwest: New Mexico, Oklahoma, Texas

U.S. Territories and Possessions

Upper Plains: Montana, North Dakota, South Dakota

West: Arizona, California, Nevada

Western Great Lakes: Illinois, Minnesota, Wisconsin

ILLINOIS

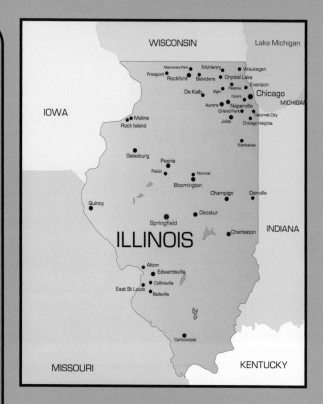

Illinois at a Glance

Area: 57,914 sq miles (149,997 sq km).[1] 25th largest state
  Land: 55,519 sq mi (143,794 sq km)
  Water: 2,395 sq mi (6,203 sq km)
Highest elevation: Charles Mound, 1,235 feet (376 m)
Lowest elevation: Mississippi River at Cairo, 279 feet (85 m)

Statehood: December 3, 1818 (21st state)
Capital: Springfield

Population: 12,880,580 (5th largest state)[2]

State nickname: the Prairie State
State bird: cardinal
State flower: violet

[1] *U.S. Census Bureau*
[2] *U.S. Census Bureau, 2014 estimate*

Illinois

A few years ago, the Associated Press examined U.S. Census Bureau *data* from all 50 states. The AP looked at the racial makeup of each state's population. It looked at the average income of residents. It looked at their average age. It looked at where they lived—whether in an urban, suburban, or rural area. It looked at their educational levels. In all, the AP examined 21 categories. And it concluded that Illinois is the state that most closely resembles the nation as a whole.

That may be so. But it would be a mistake to think of Illinois as the "most average state," as one AP headline-writer proclaimed. Illinois is big and dynamic. It plays a crucial role in the country's economy.

Geography

Located in the heart of the Midwest, Illinois covers nearly 58,000 square miles (150,000 square kilometers). In total area, it ranks as the nation's 25th largest state.

Illinois is bordered by five states: Wisconsin to the north, Indiana to the east, Kentucky to the south, and Missouri and Iowa to the west. The northeast corner of Illinois includes more than 60 miles (97 km) of coastline along Lake Michigan.

Most of Illinois' land consists of *plains*. Before it was extensively settled, this land was covered with grass. This earned Illinois its nickname: the Prairie State. Thanks to the fertile soil, Illinois is today a leading agricultural state.

A small area in northwestern Illinois has large hills and valleys. Charles Mound is located there. At 1,235 feet (376 m) above sea level, it's the state's highest elevation.

The Shawnee Hills is a band of rocky uplands, *bluffs*, valleys, and woodlands. It extends across part of southern Illinois. Much of this beautiful and rugged area is included within Shawnee National Forest. It's a favorite destination for nature lovers.

Rivers run along a significant portion of Illinois' borders. The Wabash and Ohio mark the state's southeast-

 # Words to Understand in This Chapter

Algonquian—a family of American Indian languages previously spoken in the eastern part of North America.

bluff—a high, steep bank.

confederation—an alliance or union of groups.

data—factual information.

expedition—a journey undertaken for a specific reason, such as exploration.

export—to send goods to another country; a product that is sent overseas.

Jesuit—a member of the Society of Jesus, an order of Catholic priests.

locks—gated enclosures on a canal, which raise or lower vessels by changing the water level.

plain—a large area of land that is flat or rolling and has no trees.

portage—to haul a boat or boats across land from one body of water to another.

pharmaceuticals—medicinal drugs.

ern and southern limits. The Mississippi runs the entire length of Illinois on the west. Major rivers that flow inside the state include the Kaskaskia, Little Wabash, and Illinois.

The Illinois River forms the longest section of the 336-mile (541-km) Illinois Waterway. The waterway connects Lake Michigan to the Mississippi River. Completed in 1933, it also makes use of the Des Plaines, Chicago, and Calumet rivers as well as artificial canals and lakes. A system of dams and **locks** enables vessels to be raised or lowered (depending on the direction they're traveling). This is necessary because of the 163-foot (50 m) difference in elevation between Lake Michigan and the Mississippi River at the mouth of the Illinois.

Flowering redbud trees are reflected in the calm surface of Lake Marmo on a warm spring afternoon at the Morton Arboretum in Lisle. This 1,700-acre (688 ha) botanic garden includes more than 4,100 different species of trees and over 180,000 catalogued plants.

A wide range of goods, from coal and petroleum to manufactured products and grain, are transported along the Illinois Waterway on barges. Goods moved to the northern end of the waterway—Lake Michigan at Chicago—can be offloaded onto larger ships for transport across the Great Lakes and, via the St. Lawrence

Prairie grasses grow in north-central Illinois, near Franklin Grove.

Twin waterfalls crash into Tonti Canyon on a spring day at Starved Rock State Park. The park, known for its fascinating rock formations, is located on the south side of the Illinois River in LaSalle County.

Seaway, to the Atlantic Ocean and beyond. Goods moved south along the waterway can travel down the Mississippi River all the way to the Gulf Coast. There the goods can be transferred to oceangoing ships for *export*. This, for example, is what happens with much of the corn and soybeans grown in Illinois.

In general, Illinois experiences hot summers and cold winters. Precipitation is moderate to plentiful. It ranges from an average of about 32 inches (81 cm) per year in the northeastern part of the state to about 46 inches (117 cm) in southern Illinois'

Shawnee Hills. Average annual snowfall, however, is lowest in the southern part of the state and highest in the northeast, including Chicago.

History

Illinois is a French rendering of an *Algonquian* word. It described a *confederation* of Indian tribes that occupied the central Mississippi valley region. Among these tribes were the Kaskaskia and the Peoria. They lived in what is today central Illinois.

The first Europeans to make contact with these Indians, and to explore present-day Illinois, were French. In

1673, the governor of New France (Canada) dispatched a small *expedition*. Its mission was to find and chart a large river that Indians in the Great Lakes region spoke of. Leading the expedition were a fur trader named Louis Joliet and a *Jesuit* priest named Jacques Marquette. They and their men set off in canoes from the northern shore of Lake Michigan.

Joliet and Marquette reached the river Indians called "the Father of Waters"—the Mississippi—near present-day Prairie du Chien, Wisconsin. They followed the western bank of the river as far south as the mouth of the Arkansas River.

On their return trip, the explorers cut across today's Illinois via the Illinois River. They had to *portage* to reach the Chicago River, which took them to Lake Michigan.

In his official report about the expedition, Joliet urged that a French

Barges in the Illinois River above the system of locks and floodgates at Starved Rock.

settlement be established near present-day Chicago. He thought the prairie would be ideal for farming. He also recommended that a short canal be dug to link Lake Michigan to the Illinois River. Because the Illinois emptied into the Mississippi, France could use the water route to extend its control over a huge swath of territory.

But French colonial officials weren't interested in settling the region. They mostly wanted access to fur. At the time, beaver pelts were quite valuable. They were used to make hats sold in Europe.

Nine years after Joliet and Marquette's expedition, the French built a fort on the Illinois River, at a place called Starved Rock. It was supposed to protect the fur trade from disruption.

French Canadian trappers established a few small settlements in the area. The oldest permanent one, Cahokia, dates to 1699. In the decades that followed, other forts were built. Other settlements sprang up.

By the early 1700s, France claimed an enormous expanse of territory in the interior of North America. It extended from Canada in the north to today's Mississippi and Louisiana in the south. Illinois was included in this vast area.

Inevitably, France came into conflict with Great Britain as Britain's American colonies sought to expand. In 1754, a dispute over control of the Ohio River valley touched off a major war. Eventually, most of Europe's major powers were drawn into the fighting. Battles took place not just in North America but around the globe. In Europe, the conflict was known as the Seven Years' War. American colonists would call it the French and Indian War. Some Indians did fight on the French side. But others allied themselves with the British and the American colonists.

By 1763, the French and their allies had been defeated. As part of a peace treaty, France ceded to Great Britain all territory in North America east of the Mississippi River. This included Illinois.

Great Britain would soon lose most of this territory. The American

The Northwest Ordinance of 1787 established U.S. control over territory west of Pennsylvania and northwest of the Ohio River. The states of Ohio, Indiana, Illinois, Michigan, Wisconsin, and Minnesota were eventually created from this territory.

An ORDINANCE for the GOVERNMENT of the TERRITORY of the UNITED STATES, North-West of the RIVER OHIO.

colonies rose up against, and defeated, the British in the Revolutionary War. The Treaty of Paris officially ended the war in 1783. In the treaty, Britain ceded the territory north of the Ohio River and west of the Appalachian Mountains to the newly independent United States. Four years later, the region was organized as the Northwest Territory. It included today's Illinois, along with all of Ohio, Indiana, Michigan, and Wisconsin, as well as part of Minnesota.

Congress decided that new states would be created from the Northwest Territory. They would be admitted to the Union after certain conditions were met. The population of an area first had to reach 5,000 for a new territory to be created. When its population had grown much larger and it had created an acceptable constitution, the territory could apply for statehood.

Illinois Territory was created in 1809. It included all of today's Illinois, along with Wisconsin and parts of Michigan and Minnesota.

On December 3, 1818, Illinois became the 21st state. Its boundaries were the same as exist today. Kaskaskia served briefly as the state capital. In 1819, though, the capital was moved to Vandalia. Kaskaskia and Vandalia are both located in southern Illinois. At the time, that's where almost all of the state's 35,000 or so residents lived.

Gradually, though, settlers began moving onto the vast prairies of central and northern Illinois. There they found fertile land for farming. In 1839, Springfield became the state capital. It's located in central Illinois' Sagamon County.

Chicago, meanwhile, had entered a period of rapid growth. In 1833, Chicago had only about 200 residents. By 1850, the population had swelled to nearly 30,000. By 1860, close to 110,000 people would call Chicago home. The Illinois & Michigan Canal (completed in 1848) connected Lake Michigan with the Chicago River— and ultimately with the Mississippi.

This, along with the construction of multiple railroad lines, helped to make Chicago into a transportation hub. Chicago was also the nation's busiest

The Native American warrior Black Hawk (1767–1838) led his band of Sauk and Fox Indians against American troops during the War of 1812. In 1832, angry about the loss of Sauk territories in Illinois, he resumed fighting against American soldiers. This conflict, which raged from April to August of that year, became known as the Black Hawk War.

In October 1871, a fire destroyed a large part of Chicago, killing about 300 people and leaving more than one-third of the city's residents homeless.

inland port. Because goods could be moved so easily, it was an ideal location to situate factories.

In 1860, Illinois resident Abraham Lincoln—an opponent of slavery—was elected president of the United States. Southern states responded by seceding (withdrawing) from the Union. This sparked the Civil War. Though no major battles were fought on its soil, Illinois played a crucial role in the war's outcome. It was a leading supplier of wheat, corn, and livestock to feed the Union armies. More important, it contributed a quarter-million troops.

Only New York, Pennsylvania, and Ohio supplied more soldiers for the Union cause.

In October 1871, a huge fire destroyed much of Chicago. The city didn't languish in the aftermath. Instead, it experienced a building boom, and its economic importance only grew.

More than 27 million visitors flocked to Chicago in 1893 for the World's Columbian Exposition. This huge fair marked 400 years since Christopher Columbus's arrival in the New World. Visitors saw a bustling,

Chicago's O'Hare International Airport is one of the busiest airports in the world, serving more than 66 million airline passengers per year.

thoroughly modern city that rivaled any in the country.

During the 20th century, Chicago became a destination of a very different sort. Between about 1915 and 1970, more than 6 million African Americans moved from the South to cities in the Northeast and Midwest. This came to be called the Great Migration. Half a million African Americans settled in Chicago during the Great Migration. They transformed the city's ethnic makeup and culture. Before, blacks had made up only about 2 percent of Chicago's population. By 1970, a third of Chicagoans were African American.

Government

The Illinois General Assembly is the state's legislature. It's composed of the 118-seat House of Representatives and the 59-seat Senate. State representatives are elected to two-year terms. Each decade, every senate seat has two four-year terms and one two-year term. At any given time, about a third of senators will be serving a two-year term. A lottery is held every 10 years to determine the rotation of two- and four-year terms. Illinois law allows legislators to seek reelection as many times as they want.

Illinoisans elect their governor every four years. Like members of the State Assembly, Illinois governors don't face term limits.

Because of its large population, Illinois has a big delegation in the United States Congress. In addition to its two U.S. senators, Illinois sends 18 members to the U.S. House of Representatives.

The Illinois Capitol building in Springfield houses the executive and legislative branches of the state government.

Its 20 electoral votes make Illinois a major prize for candidates for president of the United States. In recent years, however, Democrats have dominated. The last time a Republican presidential candidate carried Illinois was 1988.

The Economy

Illinois is both a major agricultural and a major industrial state. Its 74,000 farms produce a wide variety of products. In 2012, according to the United States Department of Agriculture,

Farmers use a John Deere combine to harvest a cornfield in Illinois. Corn is one of the state's major crops.

Illinois ranked third among all states in total agricultural exports. Leading crops include corn and soybeans.

Illinois is a leading producer of heavy equipment. Deere & Co., headquartered in Moline, is the world's largest manufacturer of farm machinery. Peoria-based Caterpillar Inc. is the world's top manufacturer of construction and mining equipment.

In 1955, Ray Kroc opened his first franchised McDonald's restaurant in Des Plaines. Kroc eventually took over the corporation; under his leadership the McDonald's corporation expanded internationally to become the world's largest chain of hamburger fast-food restaurants. Today the corporation operates 34,000 restaurants worldwide, and maintains its corporate headquarters in the Chicago suburb of Oak Brook.

Other products manufactured in Illinois include tools, chemicals, and *pharmaceuticals*.

Illinois' natural resources include deposits of coal and oil, which are concentrated in the southern part of the state. Illinois once had thousands of coal mines, but today fewer than 50 remain active. Commercial extraction of crude oil began in Illinois in the 1890s and reached its peak from the mid-1950s to the early 1960s.

Financial services and insurance are also important to the economy of Illinois. Chicago is widely regarded as the financial capital of the Midwest.

The People

In 2014, according to the U.S. Census Bureau, the population of Illinois was nearly 12.9 million. Illinois has more people than all but four other states.

The makeup of Illinois' population closely resembles that of the United States as a whole. The census found that 77.9 percent of Illinoisans are white. That's the precise percentage of whites in the country overall. For Latinos, Asians, Native Americans, and persons claiming two or more

Northwestern University in Evanston is one of the nation's top private universities. The school was founded in 1851, and today has an enrollment of about 8,300 undergraduate students and 7,800 graduate and professional students.

Some Famous Illinoisans

Four U.S. presidents were either born in Illinois or resided in the state at the time of their election: Abraham Lincoln (1809–1865), Ulysses S. Grant (1822–1885), Ronald Reagan (1911–2004), and Barack Obama (b. 1961). First Ladies Michelle Obama (b. 1964) and Hillary Clinton (b. 1947) were also born in Illinois.

Abraham Lincoln

Social reformer Jane Addams (1860–1935), who lived and worked in Chicago, was the first American woman to win a Nobel Peace Prize.

Barack Obama

Writer Ernest Hemingway (1899–1961), a native of Oak Park, won the Nobel Prize in Literature for such books as *A Farewell to Arms* and *The Old Man and the Sea*.

Chicago-born Walt Disney (1901–1966) was the creator of Mickey Mouse, Donald Duck, and other animated characters beloved by children everywhere.

Jazz legend Miles Davis (1926–1991) was born in Alton and grew up in East St. Louis.

Oprah Winfrey's career took off when she began hosting a talk show on Chicago station WLS-TV during the mid-1980s. Today, Oprah (b. 1954) is considered one of the most powerful people in the history of television entertainment. In 2013 she was awarded the Presidential Medal of Freedom.

Oprah Winfrey

Raised in Park Ridge, Hillary Rodham Clinton (b. 1947) has been a first lady, U.S. senator, secretary of state, and presidential candidate.

Basketball superstar Dwyane Wade (b. 1982) honed his game on the playgrounds of Chicago and Oak Lawn.

races, Illinois comes within 0.7 percent of the United States as a whole. Illinois has slightly more African Americans (14.8 percent) than the nation overall (13.1 percent). It also has slightly more immigrants (13.7 percent versus 12.8 percent).

Major Cities

Gusts from Lake Michigan buffet *Chicago* frequently, and that's the most likely origin of its famous nickname, "the Windy City." But some sources offer another explanation. In the late 1800s, they say, a New York City newspaper editor coined the nickname to poke fun at Chicagoans' tendency to boast about their hometown. Whether or not that story is true, Chicagoans do have ample reason for civic pride. With some 2.7 million residents, Chicago ranks as the third largest city in the United States. It's home to about a dozen of the country's top 500 companies. It's also a major cultural center, with dozens of museums and hundreds of art galleries and theaters. Chicago is renowned for its rich tradition of blues and jazz

Historic Wrigley Field, built in 1914, is the second-oldest active Major League baseball stadium. Since 1916 it has been the home of the Chicago Cubs.

music. It has more than 550 parks and 15 miles of public beaches on Lake Michigan. Food lovers relish Chicago's signature deep-dish pizza as well as its hot dogs.

With a 2010 population of more than 197,000, *Aurora* is the second largest city in Illinois. Located about 35 miles west of Chicago, it's an old manufacturing center. Many Mexicans settled in Aurora after a 1910 revolution plunged their country into a long period of unrest. Today, more than 40 percent of the city's people are Latinos.

Rockford (2010 population:

Irish-Americans celebrate their heritage in Chicago's annual St. Patrick's Day Parade, which is held each year on the Saturday before March 17 (unless the holiday actually falls on a Saturday). Tens of thousands of people attend the event, which includes dyeing the Chicago River green.

152,891) straddles the Rock River in northern Illinois. Known as "the Forest City" for its abundance of trees, it's the county seat of Winnebago County.

Named for the early French explorer, **Joliet** is a city of about 148,000. It's located along the Des Plaines River, about 40 miles southwest of Chicago.

Naperville may be a city of more than 140,000, but residents say it exudes a small-town charm. A recent study found Naperville to be the most affluent city in the Midwest. It's located about 30 miles west of Chicago.

About 116,000 people call **Springfield**, the Illinois state capital, home. Visitors come to see the former house and the tomb of Springfield's most famous resident: Abraham Lincoln.

Located along the Illinois River, in central Illinois, **Peoria** grew up on the site of a 17th-century French fort. Today it's the county seat of Peoria County and has a population of about 115,000.

Further Reading

Jerome, Kate Boehm. *Illinois: What's So Great About This State?* Mount Pleasant, S.C.: Arcadia Publishing, 2011.

Kyi, Tanya Lloyd. *Chicago*. Toronto: Whitecap Books, Ltd., 2014.

Santella, Andrew. *Illinois History*, 2nd ed. Portsmouth, N.H.: Heinemann, 2007.

Internet Resources

http://www.state.il.us/hpa/illinoishistory.htm

Illinois History is an online magazine for young people.

http://www.illinoisattorneygeneral.gov/children/kids/factstable.html

Illinois facts and trivia, from the office of the state attorney general.

http://www.enjoyillinois.com/

Web site of the Illinois Office of Tourism.

 # Text-Dependent Questions

1. Which major river runs the length of Illinois' western border?
2. How has Illinois benefited from its location?
3. What was the Great Migration, and how did it change Chicago?

 # Research Project

Pick one of the four U.S. presidents with an Illinois connection (Abraham Lincoln, Ulysses S. Grant, Ronald Reagan, or Barack Obama). Using the Internet or your school library, find out more about the president. Write a one-page report.

Minnesota at a Glance

Area: 86,936 sq miles (225,163 sq km)[1]. 12th largest state
   Land: 79,627 sq mi (206,232 sq km)
   Water: 7,309 sq mi (18,930 sq km)
Highest elevation: Eagle Mountain, 2,301 feet (701 m)
Lowest elevation: shoreline of Lake Superior, 602 feet (184 m)

Statehood: May 11, 1858 (32nd state)
Capital: Saint Paul

Population: 5,457,173 (21st largest state)[2]

State nickname: the North Star State
State bird: common loon
State flower: showy lady's slipper

[1] *U.S. Census Bureau*
[2] *U.S. Census Bureau, 2014 estimate*

Minnesota

Minnesota is known as "the Land of 10,000 Lakes." That's a pretty big number. But it's actually an under-count. According to the Minnesota Department of Natural Resources, the state has 11,842 lakes that have a surface area greater than 10 acres (4 ha).

Geography

A tall tale says that Minnesota's lakes formed from the footprints of the giant lumberjack Paul Bunyan and his equally huge companion, Babe the Blue Ox. In fact, giants of a much different kind created many of Minnesota's lakes.

About 1.6 million years ago, a period commonly called the Ice Age began. Cold temperatures caused massive sheets of ice to form across much of the Northern *Hemisphere*. This included most of what is now Minnesota. There, the ice sometimes reached a thickness of two-thirds of a mile.

When the Ice Age came to an end around 12,000 years ago, the *glaciers* slowly receded. But the enormous forces they'd exerted for so long had transformed the landscape. The weight and movement of the ice sheets had ploughed up rock and soil,

A young fisherman proudly shows a walleye he has caught on one of Minnesota's many lakes.

Red Lake has the distinction of being the largest lake entirely within Minnesota's borders. Located in Beltrami County, in the northern part of the state, it covers more than 288,000 acres (116,550 ha). But Minnesota's portion of Lake Superior amounts to 962,700 acres (389,591 ha). Its share of Lake of the Woods, on the border with Canada, is more than 307,000 acres (124,238 ha).

leaving the land pockmarked with depressions. As the climate warmed, these depressions filled with water. That's how Minnesota got so many lakes.

In addition to its lakes, Minnesota has more than 6,500 natural rivers and

 # Words to Understand in This Chapter

coniferous—belonging to a group of evergreen trees or shrubs that produce cones.
deciduous—having leaves that fall off every year.
glacier—a large body of ice that moves or spreads slowly.
hemisphere—one-half of the globe.
Scandinavia—a region in northern Europe that includes the countries of Sweden, Norway, and Denmark.
territorial legislature—the government of U.S. land not yet been admitted as a state.

Ancient sedimentary rocks known as Sioux quartzite form cliffs above the prairie at Blue Mounds State Park. These types of rock formations are common in northeastern Minnesota.

streams. They run nearly 70,000 miles (112,000 km) in all. The longest are the Mississippi, which flows 681 miles (1,096 km) through Minnesota, the Red (457 miles/736 km), and the Minnesota (370 miles/596 km).

Minnesota covers almost 87,000 square miles (225,000 sq km). It ranks 12th among the 50 states in total area.

Minnesota borders Canada to the north. Its eastern boundary is formed by Lake Superior and by Wisconsin.

Iowa is to the south. South and North Dakota bound Minnesota to the west.

Northeastern Minnesota is a rugged area of hills and low mountains, including the Mesabi Range. The southeastern part of the state, along the border with Wisconsin, has bluffs and valleys cut by the Mississippi and St. Croix rivers. The rest of the state consists mostly of plains and gently sloping hills.

Close to one-third of Minnesota's

Minnesota borders Lake Superior, the largest of the Great Lakes. Seen here in the distance is the Split Rock Lighthouse, built in 1910 on a basalt cliff. The lighthouse ceased operations in 1969, and is now part of a state park.

 ## Did You Know?

The northernmost place in the lower 48 states is the Northwest Angle. It's separated from the rest of Minnesota by the Lake of the Woods. To get there by land, you have to cross into the Canadian province of Manitoba.

land remains forested. ***Deciduous*** forests extend northward from the southeastern corner of the state. ***Coniferous*** and mixed deciduous-coniferous forests cover much of northern Minnesota. The western part of the state is prairie. A small section of northwestern Minnesota consists of tallgrass prairie interspersed with aspen and oak woodlands.

Not surprisingly given its northern location, Minnesota has cold winters with a lot of snow. Average temperatures in January are in the low teens or, in some areas, the single digits. Average annual snowfall ranges from about three feet (91 cm) in the southwestern part of the state to about six feet (180 cm) in the north, near Lake Superior. Minnesota's summers tend to be warm, with temperature averages in the 60s or low 70s.

History

When Europeans first set foot in what is today Minnesota, the land was occupied by two Dakota (also called Sioux) Indian tribes. The Santee inhabited the eastern region, while the Yankton lived to the west. The tribes hunted, fished, and gathered wild rice, nuts, berries, and other edible plant products. They grew corn on a limited basis.

French exploration of the area around the western part of Lake Superior began in 1659–1660. Less than a dozen years later, the French signed a trade treaty with the local Indians. The French wanted furs, especially beaver pelts.

Contact with whites changed relations among Native American groups.

Statue of Paul Bunyan, mythical hero of Minnesota's lumber camps, in Memorial Park on the outskirts of Akeley.

A Dakota Sioux man attends the Mahkato Wacipi powwow, held annually in Mankato. Today, most Native Americans live on one of the four large reservations in the northern half of the state.

The Ojibwa (or Chippewa) tribe allied with the French. Firearms obtained from the French enabled the Ojibwa to push westward from the eastern Great Lakes region. By the mid-1700s, the Ojibwa had displaced the Dakota from much of what is now eastern Minnesota.

The French gave up this area in 1763. That year, France ceded all its North American territory east of the Mississippi River to Great Britain after losing the Seven Years' War. The British thus claimed possession of about one-third of present-day Minnesota.

Great Britain ceded this land to the United States in 1783, under the treaty that ended the Revolutionary War. When the Northwest Territory was organized in 1787, eastern Minnesota was included in it. In 1803, the United States acquired the rest of Minnesota from France, as part of the Louisiana Purchase.

In 1805–06, a young army lieutenant named Zebulon Pike led the first U.S. expedition into Minnesota. Pike and about 20 men traveled up the Mississippi River. They were looking for the river's source. They didn't find it. But Pike concluded a treaty with Dakota Indians the expedition encountered. The treaty allowed the United States to establish a military outpost along the Mississippi. The outpost would extend from the mouth of the Minnesota River in the south to St. Anthony Falls, about 10 miles upriver. In return, the Dakota were to be paid $200,000. But the U.S. Congress balked at that sum. The Dakota only received $2,000.

In 1820, construction began on an army fort. Fort Snelling (originally called Fort St. Anthony) stood on a bluff near the junction of the Mississippi and Minnesota rivers. In the years that followed, settlements arose near the fort. Pig's Eye was downriver and on the east bank of the Mississippi. It would eventually become the city of Saint Paul.

From the mid-1830s to the late 1840s, lands that now make up Minnesota were part of Wisconsin Territory and Iowa Territory. In 1849, after Iowa and Wisconsin had gained statehood, Minnesota Territory was organized. White settlers flocked to the region. In less than a decade, the population would swell from about 6,000 to more than 150,000. Towns, including Minneapolis, popped up all over.

In 1857, Minnesota's *territorial legislature* drafted a constitution. Residents approved it by a big margin. On May 11, 1858, Minnesota became the 32nd state.

Over the previous three decades, the U.S. government had signed a

Fort Snelling was a frontier outpost in present-day Hennepin County.

This home, built in 1835, is the oldest stone house in the state. It was the home of Henry Hastings Sibley, the first governor of Minnesota. Today, the house in Mendota is a museum operated by the Minnesota Historical Society.

The influence of Scandinavian immigrants to Minnesota is reflected in some of the state's architecture, such as this stave church in Moorhead.

series of treaties with the Native Americans living in Minnesota. The Indians ended up ceding nearly all of their traditional lands. In exchange, the government promised to set aside other, smaller areas for Indian reservations. It also promised the Indians annuities (annual payments). But the United States repeatedly failed to live up to its treaty obligations.

By 1862, the Dakota were desperate. They now lived on a small reservation along the Minnesota River in the western part of the state. White loggers and settlers had greatly reduced the animal population in the area. This made it hard for the Dakota to get enough food by hunting. At the same time, the government hadn't paid the annuities that were promised, so the Dakota couldn't buy supplies. As a result, they faced starvation.

In August 1862, two Dakota bands rose up and attacked farms, settlements, and towns. They were led by a chief named Taoyateduta. Whites knew him as Little Crow.

The U.S.-Dakota War lasted six weeks. On September 23, Little Crow's warriors were defeated at the

Sioux warriors attack the settlement of New Ulm in August 1862. The Dakota Sioux uprising forced U.S. soldiers and resources to be diverted from waging the Civil War to Minnesota.

Hubert H. Humphrey (1911–1978) was an important political figure in the 20th century. His colleagues in the U.S. Senate nicknamed him the "Happy Warrior" because despite his friendly personality, Humphrey fought tirelessly for the progressive causes he believed in, such as civil rights for African Americans.

Battle of Wood Lake. The conflict had claimed the lives of more than 600 whites. Most were civilians. As many as 100 Dakota warriors died in the fighting.

Several hundred Dakota prisoners were hastily tried, convicted of murder, and sentenced to death. President Abraham Lincoln commuted, or reduced, most of the sentences. Still, 38 Dakota were hanged in the town of Mankato on December 26, 1862. It remains the largest mass execution in U.S. history.

During the last three decades of the 19th century, Minnesota's population grew rapidly with the arrival of large numbers of European immigrants. Many came from Germany or *Scandinavia*. The availability of good farmland in the state was a major attraction. And the Homestead Act of 1862 made it possible for people without much money to acquire land.

Minnesota, and especially Minneapolis, prospered as a center for flour milling. Minnesota's development was also fueled by the discovery of rich deposits of iron ore in the northeastern part of the state. The Mesabi Range has produced iron ore since the 1890s.

Government

Minnesota has a bicameral (two-chamber) legislature. The Senate has

In 2011, Mark Dayton became the 40th governor of Minnesota. He previously represented the state in the U.S. Senate from 2001 to 2007.

67 seats. Senators are usually elected to four-year terms. But in election years ending in 0 (for example, 2010), the term is for two years. This is to allow the redrawing of district lines. That occurs every decade following the U.S. census.

The Minnesota House of Representatives has 134 seats. Two House districts are included within each Senate district. House members are elected to two-year terms.

Legislative sessions last for two years. A new one begins in early January of each odd-numbered year.

Comedian and activist Al Franken was elected in 2008 to represent Minnesota in the U.S. Senate.

The state legislature meets in the Capitol building in Saint Paul. The governor and his administration also have offices in the Capitol, which was built in 1905.

General Mills, located in Minneapolis, is among the world's largest distributors of processed foods.

According to Minnesota's state constitution, the legislature must adjourn by the first Monday after the third Saturday in May. Also, the legislature may conduct regular business for no more than 120 days total in any two-year legislative session.

Minnesotans elect their governor to a four-year term. Unlike some other states, Minnesota doesn't limit the number of times the same person may serve in the office.

In addition to its two U.S. senators, Minnesota's delegation in Congress includes eight members of the House of Representatives.

The Economy

Minnesota is a prosperous state. The most recent data show Minnesotans' income to be well above the national average. Compared with the country as a whole, Minnesota also enjoys low unemployment and poverty rates.

Farmers pick and load sugar beets into a truck. Minnesota is the largest U.S. producer of sugar beets.

Agriculture is a vital component of Minnesota's diverse economy. Among the state's most valuable crops are corn, sugar beets, and soybeans. Minnesota is a leading producer of milk. It ranks among the top five states in hog production.

Minnesota has a significant food-processing industry. Flour, breakfast cereals, frozen and canned vegetables, butter, cheese, and packaged meats are among its leading products.

Minnesota's forests are an important economic resource. Forestry employs more than 16,000 Minnesotans, directly or indirectly. It contributes $16 billion annually to the state's economy. Minnesota produces

Lumbering is a major industry in Minnesota.

Minnehaha Falls in southeast Minneapolis was made famous by Henry Wadsworth Longfellow's 1855 poem "The Song of Hiawatha."

timber, wood pulp, and paper products.

By the 1980s, after a century of mining, Minnesota's deposits of high-grade iron ore were tapped out. But the Mesabi Range continues to yield an abundance of ore with lower iron content. This is refined into the high-grade ore used by industry. Minnesota produces some 40 million tons of high-grade iron ore per year. That's about three-quarters of the total U.S. output.

Minnesota has a robust technology sector. Firms located in the state manufacture an array of electronics. These include communications equipment, computer components, and medical devices.

Various national corporations are headquartered in Minnesota. Among them are major retail chains, banks, financial-services companies, and insurance providers.

The People

Ask a group of Minnesotans what they do in their free time, and chances are many will say they like to be outdoors. Minnesotans are known for their love of activities such as hiking, hunting, and fishing when the weather is warm. During the cold months, skiing, skating, and ice hockey are popular. Perhaps it shouldn't come as a surprise that health organizations consistently rank Minnesota among the healthiest states.

The U.S. Census Bureau estimated in 2014 that there are 5,457,173 Minnesotans. That makes Minnesota the 21st largest state by population.

Racially and ethnically, Minnesota is less diverse than the nation as a whole. According to the Census Bureau, 86.5 percent of Minnesota's

Some Famous Minnesotans

Born in Saint Paul, writer F. Scott Fitzgerald (1896–1940) is best known for *The Great Gatsby*. High school students still read the 1925 novel today.

Actress Judy Garland (1922–1969), born Frances Ethel Gumm in Grand Rapids, followed the yellow brick road to Oz, and to Hollywood stardom.

Generations of American kids have grown up with Charlie Brown, Lucy, Snoopy, and the other "Peanuts" characters. They are the creations of Minneapolis-born cartoonist Charles Schulz (1922–2000).

Singer-songwriter Bob Dylan (b. 1941), born Robert Zimmerman in Duluth, has been a music icon since the 1960s.

Minneapolis native Prince Rogers Nelson, better known as Prince (b. 1958), is a Rock and Roll Hall of Fame member with 10 platinum albums to his credit.

In 2010, Lindsey Vonn (b. 1984), the pride of Saint Paul, became the first American woman to win an Olympic gold medal in downhill skiing.

Prince

Lindsey Vonn

people are white, compared with 77.9 percent of the United States overall. African Americans make up 13.1 percent of the U.S. population, but just 5.5 percent of Minnesota's population. Nearly 17 percent of all Americans are of Hispanic or Latino heritage. In Minnesota, the figure is just under 5 percent. The proportion of Minnesotans born in a foreign country is also considerably less than the national average.

Major Cities

With a population of more than 380,000, *Minneapolis* is Minnesota's largest city. It's dotted with lakes—more than 20 lie within the city

This view of downtown Minneapolis shows the Third Avenue Bridge over the Mississippi River.

Skyline of Saint Paul, which is located downriver from Minneapolis. Both were established in the 1830s, and their proximity and shared history has led to the nickname "Twin Cities."

limits—and cut through by the Mississippi River. A center of commerce and culture, Minneapolis features a downtown of gleaming high-rises. Some of the buildings are connected by enclosed glass skywalks. This allows visitors to enjoy downtown attractions in comfort during the cold winter months.

Located just to the east of Minneapolis is Minnesota's second largest city, **Saint Paul** (population: 285,000). It's Minnesota's capital city and a business center in its own right.

Mist rises from Lake Superior near Duluth, a major port.

Because of their close proximity, Minneapolis and Saint Paul are known as the Twin Cities. More than 6 in 10 Minnesotans live in the Minneapolis–Saint Paul metropolitan area.

Rochester, the county seat of Olmsted County, is home to the world-famous Mayo Clinic. More than 107,000 Minnesotans call Rochester home.

Located at the western tip of Lake Superior, *Duluth* is a major port. Goods shipped from Duluth make their way across the Great Lakes and, via the St. Lawrence Seaway, to the Atlantic Ocean. Duluth has a population of more than 86,000.

Further Reading

Dregni, Eric. *Weird Minnesota: Your Travel Guide to Minnesota's Local Legends and Best Kept Secrets*. New York: Sterling, 2006.

Risjord, Norman K. *A Popular History of Minnesota*. Saint Paul: Minnesota Historical Society Press, 2005.

Treuer, Anton. *Ojibwe in Minnesota*. Saint Paul: Minnesota Historical Society Press, 2010.

Internet Resources

http://www.mnhs.org/

The home page of the Minnesota Historical Society.

http://usdakotawar.org/

This interactive Web site examines the U.S.-Dakota War of 1862, including its causes and consequences.

http://www.exploreminnesota.com/index.aspx

The Web site of Minnesota's state tourism agency features places and events of interest in the North Star State.

Much of Minnesota is forested or covered with lakes or small rivers like the one pictured here.

The Spoonbridge and Cherry at the Minneapolis Sculpture Garden, one of the largest urban sculpture gardens in the country.

 # Text-Dependent Questions

    1. What were the causes of the U.S.-Dakota War of 1862?

    2. Name five products of Minnesota.

    3. Which of the Great Lakes does Minnesota border? Which major Minnesota port city is located along that lake?

 # Research Project

The Homestead Act of 1862 attracted throngs of settlers to frontier areas of the country, including Minnesota. Using the Internet or your school library, research the Homestead Act. Find out what the law required settlers to do in order to make a land claim. See if you can find first-hand accounts of 19th-century homesteaders.

Visitors wade through Lake Itasca in north-central Minnesota. This glacial lake is considered the primary source of the Mississippi River.

WISCONSIN

1848

Wisconsin at a Glance

Area: 65,496 sq miles
  (169,633 sq km)[1]
  23rd largest state
  Land: 54,158 sq mi (140,269 sq km)
  Water: 11,338 sq mi (29,365 sq km)
Highest elevation: Timms Hill, 1,951
  feet (595 m)
Lowest elevation: shoreline of Lake
  Michigan, 579 feet (177 m)

Statehood: May 29, 1848 (30th state)
Capital: Madison

Population: 5,757,564 (20th)[2]

State nickname: the Badger State
State bird: robin
State flower: wood violet

[1] *U.S. Census Bureau*
[2] *U.S. Census Bureau, 2014 estimate*

Wisconsin

W isconsin's state *motto* is Forward. That seems fitting. Wisconsin pioneered a number of *progressive* policies that the rest of the country would later adopt.

Geography

The same Ice Age conditions that shaped Minnesota's terrain also shaped much of Wisconsin's. Wisconsin, too, has thousands of lakes. Most are small. The largest lake that lies completely within the state is Lake Winnebago. It covers more than 135,000 acres (54,632 ha). At about 23,000 acres (9,308 ha), manmade Petenwell Lake is the next largest. It was created in 1948 by a dam across the Wisconsin River.

The Wisconsin is the state's longest river. It runs 430 miles (692 km). The river begins in the northern part of the state and flows southwest. It empties into the Mississippi River near the city of Prairie du Chien. The Mississippi forms about 200 miles (322 km) of Wisconsin's western border. The St. Croix River forms another 165 miles (266 km) of that border. The 180-mile (290-km) Chippewa River cuts across northwestern Wisconsin before emptying into the Mississippi.

Wisconsin covers more than 65,000 square miles (169,000 sq km). In total area, it ranks as the 23rd largest state.

On its north, Wisconsin borders Lake Superior and the Upper Peninsula of the state of Michigan. Wisconsin's entire eastern border is formed by Lake Michigan. Illinois is to the south, and Iowa is to the southwest. Minnesota borders Wisconsin on the west.

Wisconsin's terrain is varied. Rolling hills, ridges, and lowlands cover most of the eastern part of the state. These features extend from the Illinois border in the south to the Green Bay area in the north.

An upland region extends about the same distance south to north in the western part of Wisconsin. Its elevation is up to 200 feet (61 m) higher

 # Words to Understand in This Chapter

communist—a follower of a political and economic system that calls for the banning of private property, among other things.

militia—an organized group of civilians who are called on to take up arms during a time of military emergency.

monopoly—control of an industry by a single company or group; a company or group that has such control.

motto—a short expression that serves as a guiding principle.

pension—a sum of money paid regularly to a retired worker.

progressive—making use of new ideas; forward looking.

Progressive Era—a period of widespread social and political reform in the United States, which lasted from the 1890s to the 1920s.

workers' compensation—a system of insurance that pays money to workers who are injured while on the job.

than that of the eastern region. This region contains some of Wisconsin's most dramatic landscapes, including high ridges, narrow valleys, bluffs, and rugged gorges carved by rivers.

Across the middle of Wisconsin, running from west to east in the shape of a jagged crescent, is a region called the Central Plain. Much of it is flat and sandy. But there are rolling, forested hills in the western part. The Central Plain contains many farms.

Most of the northern third of Wisconsin is a highland region. It has the highest average elevation in the state. It also has the state's highest point: Timms Hill, in Price County, which rises 1,951 feet (595 m) above sea level. Much of the highland region is heavily forested.

A narrow lowland area 5 to 20 miles (8 to 32 km) wide abuts Lake Superior in the far northern part of Wisconsin. The land rises gently southward, either from the water's edge or from cliffs overlooking the lake. The Apostle Islands, a group of 22 scenic islands in Lake Superior, are also part of Wisconsin.

The majestic Big Manitou Falls is located on the Black River about 13 miles (21 km) south of Lake Superior. The water drops 165 feet (50 m), making it the highest waterfall in Wisconsin.

Wisconsin's climate is generally pleasant from the late spring to the late fall. Average high temperatures in

Sailboats ply Lake Superior near the Bayfield Peninsula. Visitors to the area can enjoy the Apostle Islands, a group of 22 islands in Lake Superior that are preserved as a national park.

the summer months are in the 70s or low 80s for much of the state. Precipitation is moderate.

Winter, especially in the northern part of the state, is a different story. Temperatures of –30° Fahrenheit (–34° Celsius) or lower are recorded every year. Snowfall averages 50 to 60 inches (127 to 152 cm) in much of the state but ranges from 100 to 160 inches (254 to 406 cm) in the north.

History

Before the arrival of whites, various Native American groups occupied the land that is now Wisconsin. These include the Ojibwa, Menominee, Potawatomi, and Ho-Chunk.

Jean Nicolet is believed to be the first European to explore Wisconsin. In 1634, the Frenchman canoed across Lake Michigan and into Green Bay. He landed at Red Banks, near the present-day city of Green Bay.

A pair of French fur traders, Sieur de Groseilliers and Pierre Radisson, arrived two decades later. On two separate trips, they explored the area around Green Bay and the area around Chequamegon Bay, on Lake

The Ho-Chunk (also known as Winnebago) were among the first known inhabitants of what is now Wisconsin. These Ho-Chunk were photographed during the 1860s.

Superior. Indians told them of a great river nearby.

This information would lead to Louis Joliet and Jacques Marquette's 1673 expedition. They canoed into Green Bay, then paddled up the Fox River. After portaging, they put their canoes into the Wisconsin River. On June 17, a month after setting out, they reached the Mississippi near present-day Prairie du Chien.

Reports of Joliet and Marquette's expedition drew other French explor-

The French explorers Jacques Marquette and Louis Joliet explored president-day Wisconsin by canoe in 1673.

ers and fur traders to Wisconsin. But the French still hadn't established any permanent settlements by the time the British took control of the area in 1763, after the Seven Years' War.

On paper, Wisconsin passed to the United States in 1783. But the British retained actual control until after the War of 1812.

Between 1787 and 1836, Wisconsin was part of the Northwest Territory, Indiana Territory, Illinois Territory, and Michigan Territory. Wisconsin Territory was created on April 20, 1836. At the time, there were fewer than 12,000 settlers in the territory. By 1846, the territory's population would top 155,000.

In previous decades, Wisconsin's Indians had given up much of their

traditional lands to the U.S. government in a succession of treaties. One disputed treaty sparked the Black Hawk War in 1832. In that war, a band of Sauk and Fox Indians led by a chief named Black Hawk were defeated by U.S. Army soldiers and *militia* forces. In the aftermath of the war, other Indians concluded that they couldn't resist the U.S. government. They gave up their remaining lands.

In March 1848, voters in Wisconsin approved a constitution. Two months later, on May 29, Wisconsin became the 30th state. Madison served as the capital.

In the decades that followed statehood, Wisconsin welcomed large numbers of transplanted New Yorkers and New Englanders. The state also saw heavy immigration from Germany, Scandinavia, England, Ireland, and Scotland. Many of the newcomers were farmers. Toward the end of the 1800s, large numbers of immigrants also arrived from Poland.

Wisconsin's population had surpassed 2 million by 1900. That year, voters for the first time elected a per-

Robert M. La Follette (1855–1925), pictured here giving a radio address, was an influential governor and U.S. senator during the early 20th century.

son born in Wisconsin to serve as the state's governor. His name was Robert M. La Follette Sr. "Fighting Bob," as he was known, spearheaded a number of reforms. Primary elections were instituted, giving Wisconsin voters more power to choose the officials who would represent them. *Monopoly* businesses were broken up. Forested land was preserved.

La Follette served as Wisconsin's governor until 1905. In 1906, he became a U.S. senator. He served in the Senate, and was a leading figure of America's ***Progressive Era***, until his death in 1925.

Over the years, Wisconsin either pioneered or was among the first states to adopt a variety of important reforms. It passed some of the first laws regulating factory safety. It was among the first states to institute a ***workers' compensation*** program, which helped people injured on the job. In 1925, a decade before the country's Social Security system was

Wisconsin's natural features include extensive forested areas and more than 8,500 lakes. Both can be seen at Devil's Lake State Park in the south-central part of the state, near the city of Baraboo.

The dome of the state Capitol building rises over the Madison skyline.

created, Wisconsin became just the third state to set up a *pension* system for old people. In 1932, it enacted the country's first unemployment compensation program.

During the 1950s, Wisconsin's reputation as a bastion of progressive politics took somewhat of a hit. Joseph McCarthy, a U.S. senator from Wisconsin, led a nasty and dishonest campaign to root out supposed *communists* in the U.S. government, the army, and the entertainment industry. His career ended in disgrace.

Government

Wisconsin has a bicameral legislature. The lower house, called the Assembly, has 99 members. They serve two-year terms.

The legislature's upper house is the 33-seat Senate. Senators serve four-year terms. Every two years, half of the Senate seats are contested. Members of the Senate and the Assembly may stand for election as many times as they want.

Wisconsin's governor is elected to a four-year term. There is no limit on the number of terms one person may serve in the office.

Wisconsin sends eight members to the U.S. House of Representatives. As of 2014, both of Wisconsin's U.S. senators—Republican Ron Johnson and Democrat Tammy Baldwin—were in their first terms.

The Economy

Wisconsinites proudly call themselves "Cheeseheads." The reason is simple: Wisconsin produces a whole lot of cheese—close to 2.8 billion pounds per year. That's more than any other state. In fact, it's over one-quarter of all the cheese produced in the entire country.

It takes a huge amount of milk to keep Wisconsin's more than 120 cheese plants running. That milk

Wisconsin dairy farms like this one produce more than 27 billion gallons of milk a year, according to the U.S. Department of Agriculture. The state accounts for roughly 14 percent of the nation's total milk production.

German immigrants who settled in Wisconsin brought a tradition of beer making to the region, and brewing soon became an important industry. Milwaukee was once known as the "beer capital of the world." Today, the Miller Brewing Company, located in Milwaukee, is the largest beer brewer still headquartered in the state.

A worker measures the temperature of a vat during the cheese production process. Wisconsin produces more cheese than any other state.

comes from the state's many dairy farms. Wisconsin ranks second among all states in total milk production. It also ranks second in butter production. Dairy is the largest segment of Wisconsin's agricultural sector.

Wisconsin farmers also grow a variety of crops. These include beans, beets, corn, oats, peas, and potatoes. Wisconsin is also a leading producer of cranberries. Other important fruit crops are apples and strawberries.

Wisconsin has a significant manufacturing sector. Among its products are trucks, motorcycles, boat engines, and power tools. Wisconsin tops all other states in the production of paper products.

Tourism is a major industry in Wisconsin. Recent studies indicate that it contributes more than $18 billion annually to the state's economy. At least 180,000 Wisconsinites work in jobs supported by tourism.

 Did You Know?

Wisconsin has nearly 1.3 million dairy cows. That's about one cow for every five Wisconsinites.

The People

A few years ago, psychologists and researchers at England's University of Cambridge conducted a large survey of Americans from every state and the District of Columbia. They found that Wisconsinites were the most extroverted (outgoing) of all Americans. Residents of Wisconsin also ranked high for agreeableness—11 out of 51. Wisconsinites have a term for the way they try to interact with others: "Wisconsin Nice."

Among the states, Wisconsin ranks 20th in population. In 2014, the U.S. Census Bureau estimated over 5.7 million residents of the Badger State.

Wisconsin's population is considerably less diverse than the United States overall. More than 88 percent of Wisconsinites are white. That's 10 percent higher than the national figure.

Ice fishing is a popular pastime in northern Wisconsin.

Some Famous Wisconsinites

Author Laura Ingalls Wilder (1867–1957) wrote about the Wisconsin homesteading experiences of her family in *Little House in the Big Woods*.

Widely considered America's greatest architect, Frank Lloyd Wright (1867–1959) spent his youth in the Badger State before going on to design New York City's Guggenheim Museum, Fallingwater, and other masterpieces.

Iconic artist Georgia O'Keeffe (1887–1986) grew up on a farm in Sun Prairie.

Kenosha-born actor, director, and writer Orson Welles (1915–1985) created what some film critics consider the greatest motion picture of all time, *Citizen Kane*.

Frank Lloyd Wright

Born and raised in Waukesha, guitarist Les Paul (1915–2009) helped pave the way for rock 'n' roll by inventing a solid-body electric guitar.

Madison native Eric Heiden (b. 1958) won five gold medals in speed skating at the 1980 Winter Olympics.

Beloit-born Danica Patrick (b. 1982) is one of the most successful female race car drivers ever.

Danica Patrick

Replica of the log cabin where Laura Ingalls Wilder was born near Pepin, Wisconsin in 1867. She would later write about her Wisconsin childhood in the book Little House in the Big Woods. *Published in 1932, it was the first of a series of books she wrote about her life in a 19th-century pioneer family.*

Iconic Bascom Hall, built in 1857, is one of the oldest buildings on the campus of the University of Wisconsin in Madison. The university enrolls nearly 30,000 undergraduate students, while more than 8,700 are enrolled in graduate programs.

The percentage of African Americans in Wisconsin's population is half what it is in the entire country. The same is true for Asian Americans. Nearly 17 percent of Americans are Latinos, but just 6.2 percent of Wisconsinites are.

Major Cities

With a population of nearly 600,000, *Milwaukee* is Wisconsin's largest city. It's located on the shores of Lake Michigan, where three rivers—the Menomonee, Kinnickinnic, and Milwaukee—meet. Milwaukee is a business center. Five of the top 500 U.S. companies have their headquar-

ters in the city. At one time, Milwaukee had four major breweries and produced more beer than any other place in the world. Now only the

 Did You Know?

Fans own the National Football League's Green Bay Packers. They buy shares of stock in the team. It's not a moneymaking investment, though. Unlike regular stock, Packers shares pay no dividends and cannot be sold for a profit.

Milwaukee, the largest city in Wisconsin, is an important center for industry and manufacturing.

Miller Brewing Company remains, but it employs a couple thousand workers.

Madison, the state capital, is located in south-central Wisconsin's Dane County. Its population is more than 235,000. Four lakes connected by the Yahara River lie in and around Madison. The city's downtown sits between two of these lakes. In addition to serving as Wisconsin's capital, Madison is a county seat and a big college town. The University of Wisconsin-Madison has more than 40,000 students and faculty.

The Dells of the Wisconsin River is a five mile (8 km) long gorge noted for its scenic beauty and its dramatic sandstone rock formations.

Located along the southern shore of the bay for which it's named, **Green Bay** is a city of close to 105,000 people. It's the county seat of Brown County. But what Green Bay is most famous for is its passion for the hometown football team, the Packers.

Kenosha, a city of 100,000, sits on the shore of Lake Michigan just a few miles north of the border with Illinois. Kenosha is about 35 miles (56 km) south of Milwaukee.

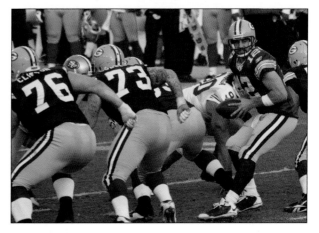

Green Bay Packers quarterback Aaron Rodgers (12) takes the snap during a game at Lambeau Field. The Packers are one of the National Football League's oldest and most storied franchises. They have won 13 NFL championships—more than any other NFL team—and four Super Bowls, most recently in 2011.

Further Reading

Heos, Bridget. *Wisconsin: Past and Present*. New York: Rosen, 2009.

Rechner, Amy. *Wisconsin: The Badger State*. Minneapolis: Bellwether Media, 2013.

Zelenyj, Alexander. *Marquette and Jolliet: Quest for the Mississippi*. St. Catharines, Ontario: Crabtree Publishing, 2006.

Internet Resources

http://www.wisconsinhistory.org/

The Wisconsin Historical Society's Web site offers a wealth of fascinating material, including articles, old images, and excerpts from historic diaries.

http://www.travelwisconsin.com/

Wisconsin's official travel and tourism Web site.

http://www.wisconsin.gov/state/core/wisconsin_facts.html

Check out the online version of *Wisconsin Natural Resources* magazine.

 # Text-Dependent Questions

1. Which of the two Great Lakes does Wisconsin border?
2. Identify at least three products that are important to Wisconsin's economy.
3. Estimate what percentage of Wisconsin's residents live in Milwaukee. Use a calculator to check how accurate your estimate was.

 # Research Project

Learn more about the Progressive Era. Compile a list of the major social and political reforms that occurred during this period.

Index

Numbers in **bold italics** refer to captions.

Series Glossary of Key Terms

bicameral—having two legislative chambers (for example, a senate and a house of representatives).

cede—to yield or give up land, usually through a treaty or other formal agreement.

census—an official population count.

constitution—a written document that embodies the rules of a government.

delegation—a group of persons chosen to represent others.

elevation—height above sea level.

legislature—a lawmaking body.

precipitation—rain and snow.

term limit—a legal restriction on how many consecutive terms an office holder may serve.